Wings of Hope

The U.S. Air Force and Humanitarian Airlift Operations

Daniel L. Haulman

Air Force History and Museums Program
1997

TABLE OF CONTENTS

Page

C–47s unloading on the ramp at Templehof Airport.

WINGS OF HOPE
The U.S. Air Force and Humanitarian Airlift Operations

The victims of recent wars and atrocities in Somalia, Bosnia-Herzegovina, and northern Iraq have captured the world's attention. The United States has responded to their cries for help by carrying out humanitarian relief operations to these and other areas devastated by natural or man-made disasters. The compassionate codenames chosen by U.S. policy-makers for these operations—Provide Comfort, Provide Hope, Provide Promise, Provide Relief, and Restore Hope—signify the nation's determination to alleviate the suffering of those less fortunate than itself. On the heels of its spectacular and decisive role in the Gulf War, the United States Air Force has demonstrated its immense capability to airlift tons of supplies and personnel in a wide variety of highly significant relief efforts.

Operation Provide Comfort delivered relief supplies to Kurdish refugees.

The Beginnings of Humanitarian Airlift

The Air Force's humanitarian operations received wide attention during the 1990s, as they will for years to come. They are part of a well-established tradition dating back three-quarters of a century to the early days of military flight.

The nation's first airmen recognized early on aviation's potential for alleviating the effects of natural disasters. As early as September 1919,

Military Airlift Command's C–5s helped deliver relief supplies to Kurdish refugees in northern Iraq in Operation Provide Comfort in mid-1991.

Army Air Service planes from Kelly Field, Texas, dropped food supplies to marooned flood victims along the Rio Grande. On a few occasions during the 1920s, American aviators bombed their own country—for good cause. They delivered ordnance against ice jams in the Delaware, Platte, and Susquehanna rivers to prevent flooding, save bridges, and restore navigation.[1] In March 1929 at least twenty-one airplanes from Maxwell Field, Alabama, delivered twenty-seven tons of food and other supplies to flood victims in the southern part of the state.[2]

The Army flew several dramatic relief missions during the 1930s. In 1932 bombers dropped supplies to Navajo Indians who had become snowbound by severe blizzards in Arizona.[3] In December 1935 the 5th Bombardment Group bombed the Mauna Loa volcano, diverting its lava flow away from Hilo, Hawaii.[4] In 1936 Air Corps squadrons flew food and other supplies to flood victims in Pennsylvania and the following year to southern Illinois.[5] During February 1939 the Army air-delivered medical aid in the wake of an earthquake in Chile.[6]

World War II proved the most costly conflict in history. It has been estimated that during the six years of warfare, about 85 million people were killed and another 60 million rendered homeless.[7] Around the globe, staggering numbers of unfortunates needed food and medical relief.

The Army Air Forces, while contributing to the Allied victory in every theater of the war, also flew vital humanitarian missions. In September 1944 the AAF began flying food into France, a country whose national transportation system had become virtually unusable and whose gross national product by 1945 had dropped to less than half of its prewar level.[8] The Netherlands had been one of the world's most prosperous countries since the seventeenth century, but the war inflicted terrible hardships on this small land. Occupying German forces opened the sluice gates of dikes and caused huge floods. In "Operation Chowhound," flown during the last month of the war in Europe, Army aviators brought food to Dutch civilians.[9]

Post-World War II through the Korean War, 1945-1953

Soon after the defeat of the Axis powers, fundamental differences between the United States and the Soviet Union in ideology, economics, and foreign policy—which had been muted by the two allies during the war—came into sharp relief. The two powers entered a period of international tension that came to be known as the Cold War.

In 1947 communists fomented a civil war in Greece and President Harry Truman sent several hundred million dollars in aid to that nation and Turkey. The United States offered far greater assistance in the Marshall Plan, announced the following year. This economic effort helped Western Europe recover from its wartime devastation and build a prosperity that blunted the appeal of communism. The United States also responded to the challenges posed by the Soviet Union during the late 1940s by extensively reorganizing the Defense Department. It was during this period, in September 1947, that the United States Air Force emerged as an independent service, separate from the Army.[10]

In February 1948 the communists seized power in Czechoslovakia by a coup and in June of that year the Soviet Union tried to sever Berlin from the Western powers. At the end of World War II, the victorious allies had reached an agreement about the division of Germany, under which the United States, Great Britain, and France occupied three western zones, which eventually became the Federal Republic of Germany, or West Germany, and the Soviet Union occupied an eastern zone, which eventually became the Peoples Democratic Republic of Germany, or East Germany. Berlin lay within the Soviet zone and was similarly divided into zones of occupation by the same four powers. The agreement assured the three Western nations access to the city along the autobahns which ran through the Soviet zone.

The Soviets reneged on this agreement and in June 1948 closed the overland routes into Berlin. Communist demonstrators drove out the elected members of the city assembly. For the next few months, the various functions of the local government were divided between east and west.

These developments led to the first humanitarian airlift of the Cold War, and the largest in history. On June 28 President Truman decided, as Secretary of Defense James Forrestal recalled his words: "We [are] going to stay[,] period." The United States Air Force began flying Operation Vittles, which became known as the Berlin Airlift. More than 300

A Berlin Airlift C–54 flies over a group of interested German bystanders.

American aircraft shuttled over 1,500,000 tons of food, medicine, coal, and other supplies into the Western sector of the capital city. The Royal Air Force contributed 101 airplanes and other support to this massive effort. The Western allies sustained the Berlin Airlift for 462 days, making almost 190,000 flights. In September 1949 the Soviet Union finally conceded that its blockade had failed, and lifted it.[11]

The significance of the Berlin Airlift in international politics can hardly be exaggerated. Operation Vittles preserved West Berlin, a thorn in the side of East Germany, and contributed to German reunification under a democratic government in 1990. This historic effort proved that an airlift alone could sustain a large population which was completely surrounded by hostile forces. Operation Vittles also demonstrated America's commitment to defend the "free world" from communist expansion. Finally, the Air Force sustained the Berlin Airlift at the same time that negotiations were underway to create the North Atlantic Treaty Organization, and the successful operation provided a compelling example of the ability of the Western allies to work together.

This C–54 commemorated the achievements of the Berlin Airlift.

After this wrenching crisis over Berlin, Cold War tensions extended into the early 1950s, as the Soviet Union continued to pursue a belligerent foreign policy. On September 22, 1949, President Truman announced that the Soviets had tested an atomic bomb. Few American officials had expected the Soviets to develop this weapon so quickly. After learning of the test, Senator Arthur Vandenberg declared: "This is now a different world."[12]

Ominous developments took place in China as well. The civil war there ended in 1949 in a communist victory, and the new government soon joined the Soviets in stirring up trouble for the United States around the globe. The Cold War turned hot in June 1950 when North Korea, supplied with arms and encouraged by the Soviets, invaded South Korea. President Truman sent United States forces to defend the South, and the United Nations also called on its members to help repel the communist attack. The UN command drove back the North Koreans, but the Chinese came to their aid and the fighting seesawed down and up the Korean peninsula. After three years of bloody conflict and two years of frustrating negotiations, the communists agreed to a truce and recognized an armistice line similar to the prewar one. The intervention of the United States and the UN had saved South Korea from its neighbor's aggression.[13]

The armistice that ended hostilities included provisions for exchanging prisoners of war. In the course of "Little Switch," between April 20 and May 3, 1953, the UN released 6,670 prisoners of war in return for 684 held by the North Koreans. During "Big Switch," which began late that July, the allies exchanged 75,823 POWs for 12,773. A host of four-engined C–124s, C–54s, and C–97s, as well as two-engined C–46s and C–47s, brought these POWs home.[14]

Repatriated South Korean soldiers arrive at Freedom Village in August 1953.

During the Korean War, the U.S. carried out a dramatic humanitarian airlift in the Middle East that was necessitated by a breakdown of transportation arrangements, rather than by war or natural catastrophe. In 1952 about 3,700 Islamic pilgrims en route to Mecca became stranded in Beirut, Lebanon. Thirteen Air Force C–54s flew them to the holy city in time for their religious observances and won America considerable goodwill among Arabs.[15]

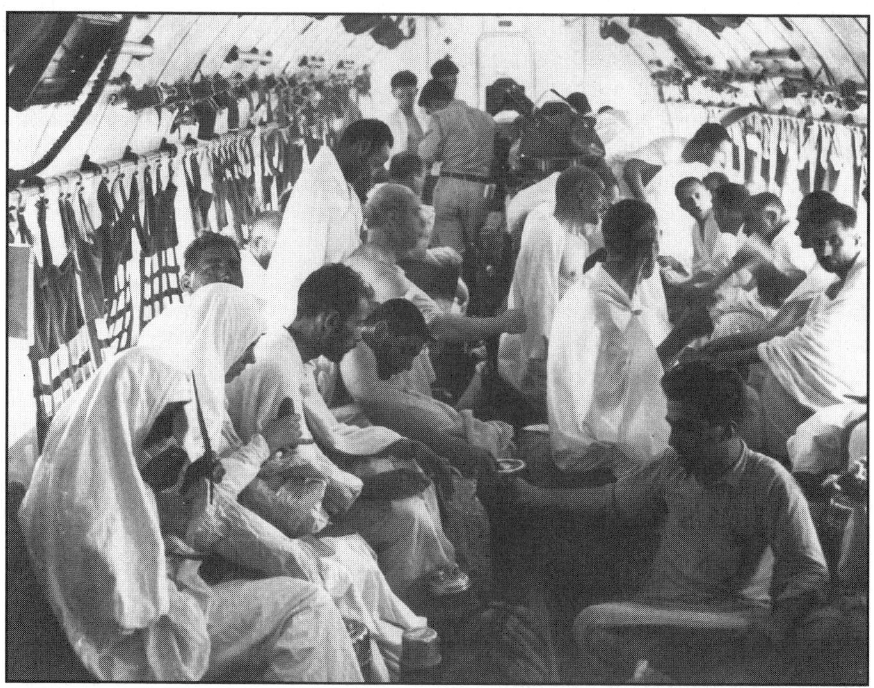

Islamic pilgrims traveling to Mecca on an Air Force C–54 in 1952.

Natural disasters the following year led to some of the largest airlifts ever flown on the Pacific Rim. In June and July 1953 floods struck Kyushu and southern Honshu, Japan, leaving more than 600 people dead, over 1,100 injured, and in excess of a million homeless. At least twenty-eight American C–119s, C–46s, and C–47s from Ashiya and Itami air bases airlifted more than 157 tons of relief cargo—including helicopters, water purification equipment, electric generators, bedding, food, clothing, and medicine—to the stricken islands. This airlift relieved the suffering of the flood victims, and also demonstrated the commitment of the United States to the welfare of Japan, which for four years had provided bases for America's Korean War operations.[16]

The humanitarian missions flown during this period did not all take place overseas. The Air Force mounted Operation Hayride, the second

Operation Hayride supplied western states snowed under in early 1949.

largest domestic airlift, in early 1949, after blizzards hit eight western states. Cargo aircraft made more than 200 flights and transported more than 4,700 tons of supplies and equipment to areas hit by the storms.[17]

From the Korean War to the Vietnam War, 1953-1965

Between the Korean and Vietnam wars, the United States Air Force flew a large number of humanitarian airlift missions. The majority were prompted by natural disasters—largely floods and earthquakes—but a few were precipitated by political crises. As during the early years of the Cold War, the Air Force mounted most of these operations overseas, although in some cases its help was called for at home.

Natural disasters and human conflicts generated several missions in 1954. That year a flood devastated India and East Pakistan, and at least twenty-seven American cargo planes transported more than 150 tons of medical supplies, bedding, food, clothing, and other items to the stricken region.[18] After the communist victory at Dien Bien Phu in the spring of 1953, the French began withdrawing their forces from Southeast Asia. During the following year twenty C–124s, C–97s, and C–118s helped airlift more than 500 wounded French soldiers from Indochina to France or to North Africa.[19]

Diplomatic events motivated other airlift operations during the mid-1950s. In May 1955 the Air Force conducted one of its most unusual humanitarian missions when it flew twenty-five Japanese women, victims of the bombing of Hiroshima, to New York for plastic surgery. This goodwill gesture contributed to the strong friendship which developed between the United States and Japan after World War II.[20]

Two major Cold War events put Air Force cargo planes into the air in 1956. In late July Egyptian President Gamal Abdel Nasser nationalized the British-controlled Universal Suez Canal Company, precipitating an international crisis that lasted through the end of the year. Twenty-four aircraft evacuated hundreds of Americans from the Middle East during this exigency.[21] In October, Hungarians rebelled against the communist regime the Soviet Union had installed in their country. Soviet tanks crushed the rebellion, driving thousands of refugees into West Germany, Austria, and Switzerland. In November and December, Air Force cargo planes brought 189 tons of food and supplies to the camps housing these fugitives.[22] By the end of June 1957, airlifts Safe Haven I and II had transported more than 10,000 refugees from Europe to new homes in the United States.[23]

Hungarian refugees arrive in the U.S. during Operation Safe Haven.

Natural disasters prompted several USAF humanitarian missions during the early 1960s. A particularly prominent example came in response to a series of earthquakes that struck Chile on May 21 and 22, 1960. The tremors, some registering more than seven on the Richter scale, produced avalanches, landslides, tidal waves, and even volcanic eruptions. Eight thousand people were left dead or missing, 5,500 were injured, and more than 240,000 were left homeless. Chile requested American assistance, and the State Department solicited a military airlift.[24] Between May 23 and June 23 Air Force transporters brought more than 1,000 tons of disaster relief equipment and supplies to the beleaguered country, in an operation called the "Amigos Airlift." The cargo included two Army field hospitals, ten Army helicopters, tents, cots, blankets, clothing, and food. Four Air Force wings based in the United States participated in the airlift, as did the service's Caribbean Command in the Panama Canal Zone. They flew a variety of transport aircraft, including two-engine C–47s and four-engine C–118s, C–124s, and C–54s, and H–19 helicopters as well. In addition to the relief cargo, the airplanes carried more than 2,400 passengers, including refugees, medical personnel, and communications specialists. Most of the flights followed a 4,500-mile, 25-hour route from various terminals in the United States to Santiago, Chile, with refueling stops in Panama and Peru.[25]

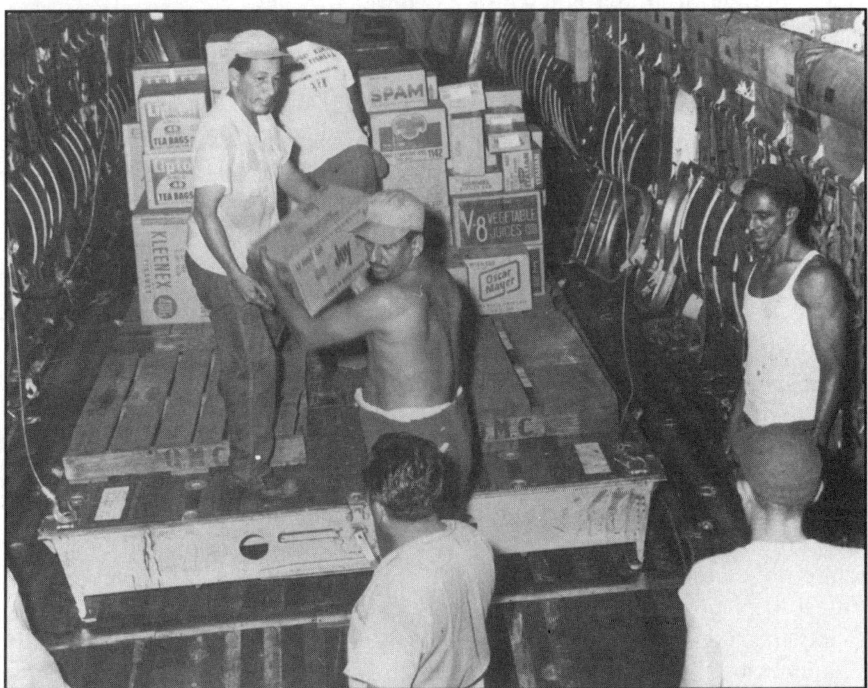

The Amigos Airlift in mid-1960 supplied food to Chilean earthquake victims.

In the autumn of 1960 a cyclone struck East Pakistan and seven C–130s and C–124s delivered eighty-nine tons of relief cargo.[26] In October 1961 two C–130s and seven C–124s transported more than 260 tons of construction equipment, sand bags, and water purification equipment to help flood victims in Cambodia.[27] Forty-seven planes delivered more than 900 tons of relief cargo to Iran after an earthquake in 1962.[28] Shortly after Typhoon Karen struck Guam the same year, that island's Andersen Air Force Base became the target of another major humanitarian airlift. Fifty transports delivered 970 tons of relief supplies and evacuated 760 people.[29] The presence of an American air force base on Guam facilitated a quick response to the devastation.

Floods prompted two significant airlifts in 1964. In the first, seven C–130s ferried 946 tons of supplies to Pakistan after a late-summer Indus River disaster brought widespread damage to the provinces of Punjab and Sind.[30] Later in the year, a fleet of helicopters, C–123s, and C–124s, as well as C–130s responded to a flood in South Vietnam. These airlifters delivered more than 2,000 tons of food, clothing, medicine, boats, and fuel, and carried over 1,500 evacuees to higher ground.[31]

During this period the Air Force flew important domestic, as well as foreign, missions. In March and April 1964 Operation Helping Hand aided victims of an earthquake in Anchorage, Alaska. At least 105 cargo planes and helicopters delivered 1,850 tons of generators, water purification facilities, construction equipment, food, medicine, bedding, clothing, and other cargo to the disaster zone. They also airlifted 850 personnel, including emergency rescue workers and evacuees.[32] Operation Biglift of December 1964 and January 1965 offered a final notable example during this period. After flooding in California and Oregon, transporters mounted 245 flights and delivered 1,598 tons of relief equipment and supplies.[33]

The Vietnam War Era, 1965-1973

During the early 1960s the United States gradually became engaged in an undeclared war in Southeast Asia. After President John Kennedy's assassination in November 1963, Vice President Lyndon Johnson succeeded him and further expanded America's military commitment to South Vietnam. As the war against the Viet Cong and North Vietnamese dragged on through the remainder of the 1960s, casualties mounted and the public became increasingly frustrated by the conflict. Domestic dissent climbed to unprecedented heights. In 1969 Richard Nixon succeeded Johnson as president and tried to address the country's frustration by "Vietnamizing" the war, shifting the burden of the combat to the South Vietnamese while withdrawing American forces. The last American units left Southeast Asia in 1973 and the tragedy culminated when the North Vietnamese overran South Vietnam during the spring of 1975.[34]

During this period the Air Force undertook not only extensive combat air operations in Southeast Asia, but also many humanitarian airlift missions. It was not surprising that the first of these involved South Vietnam. As the conflict there intensified in 1965, the number of refugees increased, and during October and November seventeen C–130s airlifted 157 tons of clothing to displaced South Vietnamese peasants.[35]

Schoolchildren of South Vietnam receive school supplies donated by citizens of Huber Heights, Ohio.

The Air Force directed several of its Vietnam-era airlift operations to Pakistan. In November and December 1970, at least seventeen C–141s and C–130s delivered over 140 tons of equipment and supplies to East Pakistan to relieve cyclone victims.[36] The following summer the airlifters were active again in the same region. Hundreds of thousands of refugees fled to India from a civil war in East Pakistan, and thirteen C–130s and C–141s brought over 2,000 tons of food, medicine, and other supplies to them. These aircraft also evacuated more than 23,000 refugees from overcrowded camps.[37] In 1973 Pakistan became the focus of the largest airlift, in tonnage, ever staged in west Asia. Two C–5s and twelve C–141s transported a record 2,400 tons of relief supplies and equipment to help flood victims.[38]

Hundreds of miles to the east, the Vietnam War came to a tragic end during the spring of 1975. When the Saigon regime collapsed, airlifters rescued tens of thousands of refugees. The mass evacuation of South Vietnam was accomplished by a complex of four overlapping operations:

Babylift, New Life, Frequent Wind, and New Arrivals. Most of the Vietnamese evacuees eventually settled in the United States. At least forty aircraft participated in the emergency missions at the end of the war. Air Force planes also delivered more than 8,000 tons of supplies to temporary refugee camps in the Philippines and on Guam and Wake islands.[39]

Refugees from South Vietnam being evacuated from Saigon to Guam aboard an Air Force C–141.

From the Vietnam War through the Gulf War, 1973-1991

Since the Vietnam War, humanitarian airlift operations have required more special equipment and increasingly skilled operators. Using modified cargo planes in a series of domestic shuttle flights, the Air Force sprayed more than 2,000 tons of fire suppressant chemicals over each of three western forest fires during the summers of 1977, 1979, and 1987.[40] The service's fire-fighting aircraft also sprayed more than 1,000 tons of chemicals over forest fires in California in August 1975 and in North Carolina in May 1986.[41]

Throughout this period, Africa remained a continent in much need of assistance. Drought and famine drew American airlifters to the Sahel region, just south of the Sahara, during the 1970s and 1980s. U.S. Air Force planes delivered large quantities of food to millions of hungry

Africans, whose plight was publicized worldwide by rock musicians who performed at fund-raising concerts.

Two of the largest Air Force humanitarian airlift operations to Africa were Authentic Assistance in 1973 and King Grain in 1974. In each instance, transporters delivered more than 9,000 tons of food to Mali, Chad, and Mauritania after a severe drought and famine. Fleets of four-engine C–130s distributed rice, wheat, flour, and powdered milk to villages in the Sahel region. The African climate prevented the planes from storing liquid oxygen for high-altitude flights, and a combination of heat, dust, poor fuel, and rocky runways multiplied aircraft maintenance problems. Yet the cargo carriers were able to deliver more than 18,000 tons of food to famine victims in less than two years.[42] In an October 1989 operation called Africa-2, an Air Force C–5 brought 250 tons of food, clothing, washing machines, and refrigerators to Chad and neighboring countries.[43]

Rollers are dragged to an Air Force C–5 in Operation Africa-2.

Asia rivaled Africa in receiving the attention of USAF airlifters after the Vietnam War. An earthquake in Turkey triggered an operation of 606 tons, carried by forty cargo planes.[44] During the Iranian revolution of 1978-1979, more than 100 C–5 and C–141 flights evacuated 5,800 Americans from that nation.[45] A much longer airlift, lasting from 1986 to beyond 1991, aided Afghan refugees who had fled to Pakistan after the Soviet Union invaded their country. During its first two years, this operation delivered more than 400 tons of relief supplies and transported over 400 injured war victims to other nations for medical treatment. By the end of 1991, the Military Airlift Command had flown over 100 missions for the Afghan refugees in Pakistan.[46] A severe earthquake struck Armenia at

An injured Afghan refugee receives assistance upon his arrival from Pakistan.

the end of 1988, and between that December and a year later, five C–5s, fourteen C–141s, and one C–9 airlifted 547 tons of tents, blankets, medicine, food, clothing, and trucks to the victims of the disaster.[47]

Much closer to home, Hurricane Hugo tore through the Caribbean in September 1989 before hitting South Carolina. In the wake of this storm, a fleet of C–5s, C–141s, C–130s, and a KC–10 made 128 flights and delivered more than 3,900 tons of relief supplies to Puerto Rico and the Virgin Islands.[48]

The Early Nineties, 1991-1994

On August 2, 1990, Iraq invaded Kuwait, its small neighbor to the south. Iraqi dictator Saddam Hussein occupied this oil-rich nation with infantry and armored units and declared it his country's nineteenth province. With Saddam's forces threatening Saudi Arabia, the USAF moved quickly. Along with the other military services, it conducted Operation Desert Shield, an enormous deployment to defend the Saudi kingdom, and President George Bush mobilized an international coalition against Saddam Hussein. The United Nations set January 15, 1991, as the deadline for the Iraqi dictator to end the illegal occupation of Kuwait. After Saddam defied this warning, almost forty nations participated in Desert Storm, the military operation which liberated Kuwait. U.S. Air Force and other coalition pilots flew a remarkably successful forty-three day air campaign, the centerpiece of the coalition's victory over Iraq in the Gulf War.[49]

In the wake of the Gulf War, Saddam Hussein brutally crushed a rebellion of the Kurds within his own country. During Provide Comfort, flown between April and July 1991, the USAF airlifted nearly 40,000 tons of relief supplies to Kurdish refugees in northern Iraq. The operation's 1,100 missions also moved more than 14,000 of these displaced people.[50]

In northern Iraq, a C–130 flies over a hastily-prepared airstrip during a Provide Comfort airlift mission.

During the Gulf War the Soviet Union offered no obstacles to American actions, because the once-dangerous superpower was now beset with severe problems of its own. In November 1989 the East German government had dismantled the Berlin Wall and accepted free travel across the city and elsewhere within East Germany. Throughout Eastern Europe, democratic governments began to replace communist dictatorships which had held power for more than a generation. Within the Soviet Union itself, an August 1991 coup by communist hardliners briefly threatened President Mikhail Gorbachev. After his reinstatement, further democratic reforms led by Boris Yeltsin spawned the dissolution of the Soviet Union and replaced it with the Commonwealth of Independent States. The Cold War ended and a new era opened in international relations.[51]

These momentous events during the early 1990s created a need for massive humanitarian operations. When the Soviet Union collapsed in 1991, economic distress threatened its citizens with malnutrition and disease, and in February 1992 the United States mounted a humanitarian airlift to help the people of this enormous nation. The first phase of this operation, called Provide Hope, delivered 2,274 tons of food and medical supplies to the former Soviet republics, with nineteen C–5 and forty-six C–141 missions flown within seventeen days. A second phase, of 182 missions, followed from late February 1992 to September 1993.[52]

Soldiers from the former Soviet republics unload medicine and supplies from an Air National Guard C–141.

An even greater tragedy befell Yugoslavia, where the collapse of the decades-old communist regime resulted in the disintegration of the country. Conflict within Bosnia-Herzegovina among Serbs, Croats, and Muslims disrupted the economy and threatened the people of Sarajevo with starvation. In response, the United States airlifted food and medicine into the Bosnian capital in an operation called Provide Promise, which began in July 1992 and exceeded the duration of the Berlin Airlift.[53] By February 17, 1993, 450 C–130 flights had brought almost 10,000 tons of relief to Bosnia.[54]

On the ground in Zagreb, Croatia, during Operation Provide Promise.

The USAF delivered large amounts of aid elsewhere around the globe. Operation Provide Relief, which took place between August and December 1992, transported thousands of tons of food to Somalia and Kenya in 1,400 C–141 and C–130 missions. This effort helped the victims of a famine caused by drought and civil war.[55] After a storm in Bangladesh in the spring of 1991, Air Force C–5s and C–141s airlifted 832 tons of relief supplies to flood victims in Operation Sea Angel.[56] After the eruption of Mount Pinatubo in the Philippines in June 1991, the USAF undertook Operation Fiery Vigil, the largest air evacuation since the end of the Vietnam War. A combination of Military Airlift Command transports and civilian airliners ferried more than 50,000 uniformed personnel and civilians from Clark Air Base and Subic Bay Naval Station to the United States.[57]

The early 1990s also offered two major examples of domestic humanitarian operations. After Hurricane Andrew hit southern Florida in late August 1992, Air Force C–5s, C–130s, and HH–60 helicopters helped bring aid to the Miami area. By September 4 they had flown more than 500 missions to the region, delivered 11,000 tons of cargo, and transported over 7,000 passengers, including military relief workers.[58] When the Mississippi River and its tributaries flooded much of the Midwest during the summer of 1993, the Federal Emergency Management Agency and the U.S. Forces Command requested airlift assistance from the Air Mobility Command. AMC employed C–5s and C–141s in more than thirty missions to deliver more than a million empty sandbags and fourteen water purification systems to Iowa, Illinois, and Missouri. The airlift helped workers contain some of the flooding and prevent the spread of disease.[59]

Wings of Hope

A review of the most significant U.S. Air Force humanitarian airlifts supports several conclusions. The airlifts were a team effort that often demanded international and interdepartmental cooperation. The governments of the afflicted nations and of the United States had to coordinate relief efforts, and the State and Defense departments had to integrate responses, often through the National Security Council. Some airlifts required the military services within the Defense Department to work together: USAF transports, for example, might carry Army helicopters, engineers, equipment, and supplies. Various major commands within the Air Force, such as the Military Airlift Command, the Tactical Air Command, the United States Air Force Southern Command, the United States Air Forces in Europe, and the Pacific Air Forces, also had to cooperate, as did the regular and reserve forces.

The airlifts also demonstrated the value of a large network of airfields, not only within the United States but abroad, in facilitating humanitarian relief. Although the sources of relief supplies were scattered across the nation, the proximity of runways made the loading of supplies easier.

Overseas facilities also proved necessary. For example, bases in Panama refueled aircraft en route to South America. Airfields did not have to be located on bases, but they had to be available to military aircraft in an emergency, and they had to accommodate those aircraft with sufficient runways and fuel. Another factor that helped the flow of relief cargo was the stockpiling of emergency supplies at certain locations. A sharp reduction in the number of U.S. Air Force bases at home and abroad could jeopardize America's ability to conduct the kinds of relief missions common during and after the Cold War. Civilian airports and airliners, already committed to busy schedules, will not be able to respond to all of the future emergencies that natural and man-made disasters will inevitably cause.

Throughout the forty-seven years between 1947 and 1994, the Cold War affected the willingness and ability of the United States to carry out relief operations. It provided large numbers of military cargo aircraft which, although designed to move troops and weapons into battle, could also transport relief supplies. America's confrontation with the Soviet Union also encouraged development of the organizational and logistical apparatus with which the United States responded to foreign emergencies, whether caused by conflict or natural calamity. Finally, the intense competition between the two superpowers for the loyalty of neutral nations encouraged participation in relief operations when natural disasters struck underdeveloped nations. Without the Cold War, the Air Force might have lacked the airplanes, bases, and budgets to conduct more than 450 humanitarian airlifts in forty years. Ironically, preparation for war has generated many of the resources used to save lives.

Humanitarian airlifts called for large numbers and varieties of aircraft. The development of larger planes allowed more tonnage to be delivered by fewer flights, and bulky equipment and large quantities of supplies necessitated the use of large cargo planes. But in many areas hit by natural disasters, small landing fields required modest-sized aircraft that were capable of landing on them. In some places, fixed-wing airplanes were unable to land at all, and helicopters were needed. If the defense budget were reduced to the point where large numbers and varieties of Air Force transports were no longer available, the United States might not be able to respond to humanitarian emergencies around the world.

The humanitarian airlifts benefited both the nation receiving the aid and the United States. The victims of disaster obviously gained from the delivery of food, medicine, clothing, bedding, shelters, and other supplies, and their governments were also able to rebuild devastated areas more rapidly with airlifted American equipment. However, the United States also profited from the airlifts by forging stronger bonds of goodwill and economic interdependence between itself and the afflicted nation, and by contributing to regional stability. Through its airlifts, the Air Force helps to insure friendly regimes in the world that will be receptive to Americans politically, economically, and militarily.

The relief operations also doubled as combat training. The delivery of hundreds of tons of humanitarian equipment, relief workers, and supplies over thousands of miles in short periods of time prepared both air and ground crews for airlifting armored vehicles, weapons, and troops in case the emergency were war instead of natural disaster. The same skills Air Force personnel applied to relieving victims of natural disasters around the world would be needed in case of a wartime emergency in those very areas. Humanitarian airlift operations are not only an alternative to combat operations, but also a supplement to them.

Above all, the humanitarian airlifts have demonstrated that Defense Department organizations have useful peacetime roles. Military operations can kill, but they also save lives; they can injure, but they also heal; they can damage and destroy, but they also repair and rebuild. America will face many enemies in the future, including natural disasters such as floods, hurricanes, earthquakes, and blizzards. The United States Air Force has a tradition of meeting these challenges. With adequate support, that tradition will endure.

Appendix

Selected U.S. Air Force Overseas Humanitarian Operations, 1947-1994
Compiled by Christopher J. Bowie

Acronyms used in descriptions: ACC, Air Combat Command; AMC, Air Mobility Command; ANG, Air National Guard; FEAF, Far East Air Forces; PACAF, Pacific Air Forces; MAC, Military Airlift Command; SAC, Strategic Air Command; TAC, Tactical Air Command; USAFE, United States Air Forces Europe.

1947

Sep	The USAF began the Post-Hostilities Mapping Project, in which reconnaissance aircraft photographed the land masses and island groups in the Pacific region from Guadalcanal to Japan.
Oct	USAF airlifters transported cholera vaccine to Cairo, Egypt, and conducted spraying operations.
Nov	A FEAF C–54 airlifted 10,000 pounds of cholera vaccine from Shanghai, China, to Jiddah, Saudi Arabia.

1948

Jan	After a fire destroyed a local warehouse in Labrador, a U.S. airlifter delivered relief supplies.
Jun	The Berlin Airlift began.

The Berlin Airlift helped keep the city in Allied hands.

Nov FEAF provided air rescue support for the flight of a British aviatrix from Chitose, Japan, to Shemya, Alaska.

1949

Jan After an outbreak of yellow fever, a B–29 airlifted 75,000 doses of vaccine to Panama.

Aug To aid earthquake victims in Ecuador, twelve C–47s transported forty-one tons of relief supplies to the affected area.

Sep C–47s delivered medical supplies to India to combat cholera and typhus outbreaks.

1951

Mar USAF aircraft delivered relief supplies to assist Japanese rendered homeless by severe earthquakes in Hokkaido.

May C–47s carried out spraying operations in locust-plagued areas around New Delhi, India.

Sep To aid victims struck by an outbreak of yellow fever in Costa Rica, a USAF C–82 airlifter and H–5 helicopter brought in medical personnel and supplies of vaccine.

Nov USAFE transports airlifted supplies and clothing to flood-stricken areas in Italy.

Nov To assist victims of a volcanic eruption in the Philippines, USAF aircraft delivered food and medical supplies.

Dec USAFE transported 2,000 pounds of clothing donated by children of Akron, Ohio, to the children of Berlin.

1952

Mar In Operation Warm Clothes, USAF airlifters delivered clothing and supplies to Japanese left homeless by an earthquake and a major tidal wave.

May The USAF sent two C–47s to India to spray insecticide where vital crops were threatened by a destructive locust infestation.

Jul After a British airliner crashed in the Mediterranean Sea, a USAF helicopter rescued thirty-two passengers.

Sep U.S. airlifters conducted relief and evacuation operations in the Pacific at Wake and Kwajalein in the aftermath of Hurricane Olive.

1953

Feb USAF airlifters assisted flood-stricken areas of the Netherlands by transporting more than a million pounds of relief supplies and evacuating people from disaster areas.

Mar After floods, six C–47s airlifted 657 tons of food and other supplies to Ecuador.

Mar USAF helicopters rescued crew members from a sinking Japanese vessel near Okinawa.

Apr	Four C–119 airlifters transported medical supplies to Turkey to provide earthquake relief.
Jun	In Operation Mercy Lift, the USAF delivered assistance to Japanese stricken by major flooding near Kyushu.
Jun	The USAF airdropped foodstuffs to Japanese victims of a flash flood at Wakayama.
Jul	After a British airplane ditched in the Mediterranean Sea, a USAF helicopter rescued all sixteen passengers.
Aug	Twenty C–119 airlifters flew 270,000 pounds of relief supplies to earthquake-stricken Greece.
Nov	The USAF delivered tons of foodstuffs to assist destitute Koreans.

1954

Jan	USAF air rescue units saved crewmen from a sinking vessel near Casablanca, Morocco.
Jan	USAFE rescue aircraft evacuated sixty-eight persons and delivered rescue personnel and supplies to avalanche-struck Blons, Austria.
Feb	A USAFE C–119 airdropped thirteen tons of food and supplies to the German island of Juist, in the East Frisian Islands.
Apr	USAF aircraft airlifted and airdropped food and supplies to flood-stricken areas around Damascus, Syria, and Baghdad, Iraq.
May	Three USAFE C–119 aircraft airlifted 21,000 pounds of food to earthquake victims at Lárisa, Greece.
Jun	U.S. airlifters conducted Operation Wounded Warrior in Indo-China, the air evacuation of 509 wounded French soldiers from Asia to France.
Aug	Seven USAF C–119s airlifted flood relief supplies to Karachi, Pakistan, and New Delhi, India.
Aug	USAF aircraft flew flood relief to citizens of East Pakistan due to serious flooding.
Sep	After floods in Honduras, ten C–47s and two helicopters airlifted fifty tons of relief supplies.
Sep	Airlifters and helicopters provided relief supplies and evacuated survivors from earthquake-stricken zones in Algeria.
Oct	USAF C–124 airlifters delivered emergency fire-fighting equipment to assist in fighting a major oil storage fire in Japan.
Oct	After Hurricane Hazel struck Haiti, a USAF rescue unit airlifted relief supplies and evacuated victims.

1955

Apr	The USAF provided assistance for Philippine citizens rendered homeless by a major earthquake.
May	USAFE airlifted food and medical supplies to earthquake-stricken Vólos, Greece.
May	In Operation Hiroshima Maidens, the USAF transported

twenty-five women disfigured by nuclear blast effects from Japan to New York for plastic surgery.

Aug USAFE airlifters brought tarpaulins to Lyon, France, to provide protection after high winds blew the roofs off several buildings.

Sep After floods in the Tampico, Mexico, area, USAF airlifters and helicopters airlifted 630 tons of relief supplies.

Oct After flooding, a USAF unit airlifted food and medical supplies to Costa Rica.

Nov TAC airlifters assisted Operation Deep Freeze in New Zealand with logistical and airdrop support. Deep Freeze supported the establishment of scientific research stations in Antarctica in preparation for the International Geophysical Year Program, 1957-1958.

Nov USAF helicopters rescued flood victims near the town of Shizunai, Japan.

Nov Due to flooding from the Magdalena River, USAF C–47s transported food and medical supplies to the stricken region in Colombia.

1956

Jan USAFE airlifted a rare drug to Italy in an attempt to save an Italian infant dying of leukemia.

Feb During Operation Snowbound, forty USAFE C–119s transported 332 tons of relief supplies for refugees in Greece and Italy.

Mar C–119 airlifters carried food and tents to Turkey following a major earthquake.

Aug USAFE airlifters delivered 34,000 pounds of relief supplies following a flash flood in Tehran, Iran.

Dec Serious crop failures in Japan led the USAF to airlift tons of rice into the famine area.

1957

Jun Airlifters brought insecticide to Tunisia and Morocco to combat a locust infestation.

Jul Flood relief supplies were distributed to victims in southern Kyushu, Japan, by PACAF H–21 helicopters.

Oct After flooding, USAF aircraft airlifted three tons of relief supplies to victims in eastern Spain.

Dec After an earthquake in Iran, USAF airlifters brought in relief supplies.

1958

Jun A PACAF C–130 airlifted 300,000 shots of anti-cholera serum from Manila, Philippines, to Bangkok, Thailand, in response to an urgent request from the Thai government.

Sep PACAF H–21 helicopters and C–47s provided Japan with airlifts of relief supplies to the typhoon-stricken Izu Peninsula and Okinawa.

Sep A USAF helicopter rescued forty-eight victims of a Portuguese shipwreck off the Azores.

Dec After flooding in Morocco, USAF helicopters assisted in evacuating flood victims in the Souk el Arba area.

1959

May As part of the People to People Program initiated by President Eisenhower, TAC C–130s airlifted food, clothing, farm equipment, livestock, and other materials to Korea and Japan.

Jun After a polio outbreak in Guatemala, a C–118 carried 25,000 units of Salk vaccine to aid the local population.

Sep PACAF H–21 helicopters rescued almost 5,000 people and C–124s airlifted relief supplies to Japan following the devastation of Nagoya by a typhoon. TAC C–130s also participated in this relief operation.

Oct Air rescue helicopters from Kadena rescued twenty-nine Japanese sailors from a foundered vessel near Okinawa.

Nov USAF airlifters brought in a 100-bed hospital to assist local authorities in Morocco in dealing with a massive food poisoning crisis.

Dec USAFE transports airlifted food and relief supplies to Fréjus, France, following the bursting of a nearby dam.

1960

Jan In response to a major earthquake in Peru, three USAF airlifters brought in fifteen tons of relief supplies.

Feb In Operation Amigo, three TAC C–130s supported President Eisenhower's trip to South America and also delivered relief supplies to Chile following a tidal wave.

Mar USAFE airlifters transported rescue workers, supplies, and equipment to the Moroccan city of Agadir in response to an earthquake.

Mar In response to flooding in northeast Brazil, six USAF C–124s brought in two rescue helicopters and 160 tons of relief supplies.

May USAF cargo aircraft airlifted over 1,000 tons of relief supplies to aid victims of an earthquake in Chile.

Jun The USAF transported livestock to a Japanese village devastated by a major typhoon.

Aug USAF airlifted iron lungs to Hokkaido, Japan, where 600 cases of polio had been found.

Sep The USAF provided supplies and other materials to Philippine citizens rendered destitute by serious flooding.

Oct USAFE C–130s delivered almost eighty tons of relief supplies to Pakistan following cyclone and tidal wave damage.

Dec When Japanese farmers suffered major livestock losses in a local flood, the USAF airlifted Jersey cows to replace their stock.

1961

Jan The USAF airlifted 4,000 pounds of clothing to help destitute Korean orphans.

Korean children smile approval at their new attire.

Jan Sixteen C–130s flew more than two million pounds of food relief to the Congo to aid famine-stricken areas.

Workers in Southern Rhodesia load corn destined for the Congo.

Apr USAFE aircraft airlifted blankets and tents to Jordan following major floods.

Apr Following major fires in Al Hudaydah, Yemen, USAFE airlifters brought in relief supplies.

Apr A USAFE airliner flew in relief supplies and carried out air rescue search operations following heavy storms around Benghazi, Libya.

Aug USAF airlifters carried 120,000 pounds of insecticide to Egypt to save the cotton crop.

Sep The USAF airlifted numerous supplies to a flooded Thai village using C–130 transports.

Oct USAF air transports delivered water purification equipment to Cambodia, where heavy rains had caused floods.

Nov Following floods in Kenya, USAFE airlifters brought in relief supplies.

Nov Following the devastation of British Honduras (now Belize) by Hurricane Hattie, U.S. airlifters brought in communications equipment to assist in relief efforts.

Nov Due to major famine, USAF airlifters provided food and supplies in response to a UN decision to send aid to the stricken Congo.

Nov USAFE helicopters flew in relief supplies and helicopters following floods in Somalia.

1962

Feb USAFE provided relief assistance to flood-stricken areas around Hamburg, West Germany. Rescue operations were carried out by six USAF C–130s and four Army SH–19 helicopters.

Feb USAF airlifted twenty-nine tons of food and supplies to the Philippines for the people of Mindanao, who were in danger of starvation because of floods.

Mar USAFE provided relief assistance to flood victims around Tripoli, Libya.

Apr U.S. transports airdropped over 1,400 tons of grain to aid 50,000 flood victims in Tanganyika.

May A C–123 returning from the United States was routed through Iran and Afghanistan to conduct aerial spraying in response to a regional locust problem.

Aug In response to floods and famine in western Colombia, USAF C–130s airlifted almost ninety tons of food and emergency supplies to the stricken region.

Sep USAFE provided airlift support to Iran after an earthquake struck. Almost one million pounds of aid, including trucks, trailers, and a water purifying unit were airlifted to the region.

Oct The USAF airlifted food for Congo inhabitants suffering from famine.

Nov In the wake of Typhoon Karen, U.S. airlifters delivered over 1,000 tons of relief supplies to Guam to assist in recovery efforts.

Nov The USAF participated in flood relief operations to Tunisia.

1963

Jan USAFE helped airlift almost 700,000 pounds of supplies and equipment plus medical teams to flood-stricken Rabat, Morocco.

Jan Four C–119s airlifted nine tons of relief supplies to Honduras.

Feb When the Ceyhan River flooded in Turkey, USAF helicopters rescued ninety persons.

Feb USAF transports and helicopters provided medical and rescue personnel, a hospital, and other supplies to Al Marj (Barce), Libya, following a major earthquake.

Feb The USAF carried out an airlift of beds, blankets, and foodstuffs to the people of Niigata, Japan, after a blizzard blocked all surface transportation to that city.

Feb A C–124 delivered foodstuffs and mail to a snowbound Korean island.

Feb After floods in southern Spain, USAF aircraft evacuated sixty-nine people.

Feb MAC C–130s airlifted 16,000 pounds of medical supplies to Jakarta, Indonesia, following a devastating flood in that area.

Mar When sustained bad weather prevented shipping to Santa Maria Island, Azores, USAF airlifters delivered food to the island.

Apr The USAF airlifted 7,200 pounds of canned food to feed starving Papuan children in the Schouten Islands, Papua New Guinea.

May To aid victims of a famine in northeastern Mexico, USAF C–119s and a C–47 airlifted seventeen tons of food and clothing.

Jul After a devastating fire, USAF C–130s airlifted 2,000 pounds of clothing for the relief of homeless Vietnamese.

Jul Twenty-five C–130s and other USAF aircraft airlifted 455 tons of relief supplies to Belgrade, Yugoslavia, to aid earthquake victims.

Jul The USAF brought nearly two tons of medical supplies to Laos to equip a hospital set up by an American volunteer physician.

Aug A TAC C–46 airlifted ten tons of medical supplies, along with researchers and medical technicians, to the village of San Joaquín, Bolivia, which was stricken by an outbreak of hemorrhagic fever.

Sep After forest fires swept through southern Brazil, a TAC C–130 delivered fifty tons of relief supplies.

Sep USAF aircraft airlifted six tons of foodstuffs to feed Korean orphans.

Oct When Typhoon Gloria devastated parts of Taiwan, USAF airlifters delivered five tons each of wheat and clothing to aid victims.

Oct After Hurricane Flora, a C–124 airlifted 385 tents and cots to aid victims in Tobago.

Nov Three C–123s sprayed 24,000 acres of crops in Thailand threatened by an insect plague.

Dec When a Greek luxury liner caught fire in the Atlantic, six USAF C–54 aircraft delivered survival kits and life rafts.

1964

Jan A PACAF C–130 delivered fourteen tons of medical supplies to Saigon, South Vietnam, from Manila, Philippines, to combat an outbreak of cholera.

Jan In response to flooding in eastern regions of Brazil, two C–124s airlifted 120 tons of relief supplies.

Jan Volcanic eruptions followed by flooding caused much suffering in Costa Rica. To assist in recovery efforts, U.S. airlifters delivered 289 tons of relief supplies and an engineering team.

Feb Medical supplies collected by U.S. civilians were airlifted to Nicaragua to support St. Luke's Clinic, the only free hospital in Managua.

Mar After a series of earthquakes in the Azores, USAF airlifters delivered sixty tons of relief aid.

Mar Two TAC C–130s supported the National Geographic Polar Expedition, delivering cargo, husky dogs, and personnel to Alert Island, northwest of Thule Air Base, Greenland.

Apr After forest fires in western Panama broke out, a C–118 brought in three tons of borax to fight the blazes.

May TAC's 1st Air Commando Wing delivered fifteen tons of medical and other supplies to Colombia for the World Medical Relief Fund.

Jun PACAF C–130s airdropped over 100,000 gallons of fire-fighting foam and other supplies to earthquake-devastated Niigata, Japan.

Jun After an epidemic in Bolivia, four USAF airlifters brought in medical personnel and supplies.

Jun USAF C–130s carried almost 1,000 tons of food to flood-stricken Pakistan, including airdrops to isolated regions, where critical food shortages had developed.

Aug After Hurricane Cleo hit Guadeloupe, a C–124 airlifted seven tons of relief supplies to the stricken region.

Sep After a severe storm in Panama, the USAF airlifted food and other relief supplies to that nation.

Oct Ten USAF C–124s and one C–130 transported tents, bedding, and 169 tons of other relief supplies to Yugoslavia.

Nov Airlifters delivered bridge materials and engineers to flood-stricken Tunisia.

Dec A PACAF C–54 delivered 4,000 items of canned food to the victims of a typhoon in Mindanao, Philippines.

Dec A USAF airlifter delivered a badly needed generator to Africa for the hospital ship *Hope*.

Dec Airlifters transported 100 tons of grain for famine victims in Somalia.

1965

Jan Airlifters delivered relief to flood victims at the Tunisian seacoast town of Zarzis.

Mar SAC tankers provided support to Royal Air Force tactical aircraft after Britain grounded its Valiant refueling aircraft, which had been struck by a catastrophic fatigue problem.

Apr After an earthquake in central Chile, four USAF C–130s airlifted fifty-five tons of relief supplies to the region.

Apr Two C–130s deployed to Somaliland loaded with food and medical supplies.

May The USAF airlifted 61,000 pounds of firefighting chemicals to combat a fire raging aboard a Norwegian tanker off Japan.

May After an earthquake in El Salvador, USAF airlifters brought in over 300 tons of relief supplies and 207 rescue personnel.

Jun USAF airlifters delivered irrigation pumps to help Korean farmers cope with a severe drought.

Aug The USAF airlifted medical equipment and twenty-five dentists aboard C–54s to aid a Japanese leper colony.

Sep USAF air transports flew relief goods to the victims of a volcanic eruption in central Luzon, Philippines.

Sep After floods in Honduras, USAF C–130s airlifted twenty-five tons of relief supplies to the area.

Sep USAF helicopters rescued forty-three people during flooding in Italy.

Nov After a fire on a cruise ship in the Bahamas, USAF airlifters transported burn specialists to the scene and evacuated burn patients to the United States for further treatment.

Dec PACAF units provided relief supplies and assistance to fire victims in Khorat, Thailand.

Dec C–130 airlifters transported tents to flood victims in Rabat, Morocco.

1966

Jan C–130s airlifted 10,000 blankets to aid victims of a fire at Misawa, Japan.

Feb Following a hurricane in the Samoa Islands, three C–124s airlifted electrical power equipment, construction materials, and foodstuffs to Pago Pago.

Mar USAF airlifters brought in twenty-five tons of milk to needy families in Ghana.

Apr USAF air transports airlifted sixteen tons of medical supplies and vaccine to help the Sudanese cope with a cholera epidemic.

Aug Airlifters brought in almost 100,000 pounds of supplies, including a thirty-six bed hospital, to aid earthquake victims in Turkey.

Sep Two C–130s brought in personnel and supplies to assist in relief efforts in Chad. The airlifters brought in more than 500 tons of wheat.

Sep The USAF participated in typhoon relief operations in Japan.

Sep Airlifters provided relief and assistance to flood victims in both Thailand and Laos.

Oct Two C–130s and a C–124 airlifted tents, food, and other relief supplies to the Dominican Republic after a devastating hurricane.

Oct Two C–130s provided assistance to Mexican officials in their efforts to recover from hurricane damage. The cargo included medicine, vehicles, and fuel.

Oct In response to an earthquake in Peru, four C–130s brought in fifty-five tons of fuel and other relief supplies.

Nov USAFE airlifters brought in over 200 tons of medical supplies and relief personnel to flood-stricken areas around Florence, Italy.

Nov In response to flooding in Panama, USAF helicopters airlifted three tons of relief supplies and 105 refugees.

1967

Jul After an earthquake in northern Venezuela, a USAF C–130 and C–54 brought in thirty tons of relief supplies.

Jul After an earthquake in Turkey, USAF airlifters brought in relief supplies.

Sep USAF airlifters conducted evacuation and relief operations after Typhoon Sarah battered Wake Island.

Sep Twenty USAF airlifters brought in 116 tons of relief supplies and 175 relief workers after floods hit Mexico.

1968

Jan USAF airlifters carried fifty-nine personnel and 168 tons of equipment to aid earthquake victims in Sicily.

Feb After floods, USAF C–130s airlifted twenty tons of relief supplies to Bolivia.

Apr To aid victims of drought, a USAF C–130 airlifted forty-six tons of food to Ecuador.

Apr After Typhoon Jean wrecked havoc on Guam, USAF airlifters brought in ninety-seven tons of relief supplies.

May USAFE airlifted 100 tons of emergency supplies for food relief in Ethiopia.

Jul After a volcanic eruption in Costa Rica, USAF aircraft airlifted twelve tons of relief supplies to the stricken area.

Aug USAF aircraft airlifted twenty-six tons of food and 260 evacuees in response to major flooding in Nicaragua.

Sep USAF C–130s airlifted foodstuffs to island inhabitants of Minami Daito, Japan, who had been cut off from ship traffic by bad storms.

Sep After Typhoon Della struck the Ryukyu Islands, four C–130s airlifted relief supplies to inhabitants.

Oct After an earthquake in Iran, two USAF C–130s airlifted fifty-seven tons of tents for homeless victims.

1969

Feb In Operation Combat Locust, three TAC spray planes deployed to Saudi Arabia to eliminate a locust plague.

Apr The USAF provided relief supplies for those injured and rendered homeless by a major fire in Rabat, Morocco.

May After an outbreak of encephalitis in Ecuador, USAF C–141 airlifters and C–123 spray planes airlifted and dispensed fifty-four tons of insecticide.

Jul A MAC C–141 airlifted a critically burned Russian sailor to Hawaii for treatment at a civilian hospital.

Jul In response to flooding and a border skirmish with Guatemala, USAF cargo planes airlifted twenty-six tons of relief supplies and equipment to Honduras.

Sep Six MAC airlifters flew in much needed food and equipment to Guatemala after Hurricane Francelia struck.

Oct Two C–130s delivered more than 164 tons of foodstuffs to famine-stricken citizens of Chad.

Nov USAF airlifters and helicopters provided rescue assistance for flood-stricken Tunisia.

Dec MAC aircraft evacuated three sick Russians in the Pacific and brought them for treatment in U.S. hospitals.

1970

Jan A C–141 airlifted relief supplies to Morocco to aid flood victims.

Jan After flooding in Costa Rica and Panama, USAF aircraft airlifted fifty-six tons of relief supplies and 576 evacuees.

Feb USAF rescue helicopters helped save crew members from two sinking vessels in the Pacific.

Mar The USAF provided relief supplies to Turkey following an earthquake in the Gediz area.

May Following a devastating earthquake in Peru, eighteen U.S. airlifters delivered 732 tons of relief supplies and transported injured locals.

Oct After flooding, three USAF C–124s airlifted more than sixteen tons of relief supplies to Puerto Rico.

Oct USAFE airlifters moved in two military hospitals and medical personnel to Amman to treat wounded following the outbreak of the Jordanian civil war.

Oct After flash flooding in northwestern Italy, a USAF C–130 delivered relief supplies.

Oct A PACAF airlift moved 375 tons of cargo and 453 people during typhoon relief operations in the central Philippines.

Nov After floods in Colombia, USAF C–130s airlifted twelve tons of relief supplies and equipment.

Nov U.S. airlifters carried relief supplies and Army forces to Pakistan to assist in relief efforts.

Dec USAF rescue units aided in rescue attempts following the sinking of a Korean ferry. Over 300 people were lost.

Dec In response to major flooding in Costa Rica, a USAF C–123 and helicopter brought in seventy-three tons of relief supplies and airlifted 279 evacuees.

Dec To aid victims of an earthquake in Ecuador, three USAF C–130s airlifted 140 tons of relief supplies.

1971

Jan PACAF airlifters provided relief to Kuantan, Malaysia, following a flood.

Feb To aid flood victims in Bolivia, a USAF C–130 brought in seven tons of Red Cross supplies.

Mar A C–141 airlifted a recently released American agricultural adviser who had been taken hostage by Uruguayan rebels.

Mar MAC airlifted approximately forty tons of relief supplies to residents of Okinawa following a devastating typhoon.

Mar In response to a volcanic eruption in Nicaragua, USAF airlifters brought in ninety-five tons of relief supplies and building material.

May Two PACAF C–130s airlifted tents to Truk Island following a destructive typhoon.

May A U.S. search and rescue unit delivered medical personnel by parachute to a Soviet freighter in the Pacific to assist a burned Russian sailor.

May USAFE C–130 sorties aided earthquake victims around Bingöl, Turkey.

Jun USAFE provided humanitarian aid to Pakistan and India to assist refugees of the East Pakistan civil war. During thirty days of operations, airlift aircraft flew in 2,176 tons of food and medical supplies and flew out over 23,000 refugees.

Jun In Operation Bonny Jack, TAC deployed three C–130s from Pope AFB to Delhi, India, with cholera vaccine on board.

Jul U.S. airlifters transported more than forty-three tons of relief supplies to aid survivors after an earthquake in Chile.

Jul USAFE airlifters flew cholera relief supplies to Chad.

Jul After floods in Mexico, USAF aircraft rescued nineteen flood victims and airlifted five tons of food and medical supplies.

Sep After Hurricane Edith devastated coastal regions of Nicaragua, U.S. airlifters transported over ninety-three tons of relief supplies to aid victims.

Sep After Tropical Storm Fern hit northeastern Mexico, USAF helicopters aided in the rescue of ninety-one persons.

Oct USAF rescue helicopters saved the crewmen of a sinking Taiwanese freighter off the Philippines.

1972

Mar In response to an earthquake and flooding in Peru, USAF C–130s airlifted 135 tons of relief supplies to the stricken area.

May USAFE airlifted to Turkey 5,000 pounds of medical equipment donated by civilians from Germany.

Jul PACAF C–130s moved over four million pounds of cargo to assist in flood relief operations in the Philippines.

Jul USAF airlifters evacuated the inhabitants of Johnston Atoll when it was threatened by Typhoon Celeste.

Aug USAF rescue units saved nearly 750 lives during heavy flooding near Seoul, South Korea.

Nov Four helicopters from Osan Air Base saved 763 Korean civilians from flood waters.

Dec Following a devastating earthquake in Managua, Nicaragua, U.S. airlifters brought in almost 2,000 tons of relief supplies and 1,200 personnel. Within thirty-eight hours, the United States delivered two mobile surgical hospitals.

1973

Jan Airlifters evacuated local residents and "rescued" 833 tons of fish-processing equipment following the eruption of a volcano in Iceland.

May TAC C–130s delivered 2,000 tons of food to drought-stricken areas in Mali, Mauritania, and Chad.

Jun After a flood in Guatemala, a USAF C–130 airlifted seven tons of tents to the region.

Jul PACAF C–130s delivered 100 tons of medical supplies to Tan Son Nhut, South Vietnam, to stop an outbreak of hemorrhagic fever.

Jul To combat an encephalomyelitis epidemic in Panama, USAF aircraft airlifted and dispensed nine tons of insecticide.

Jul Two PACAF C–47s flew to Lahore, Pakistan, for disaster relief operations. The aircraft sprayed 100,000 acres of rice fields to destroy borer worms.

Oct After a flood in northern Colombia, two C–130s airlifted sixteen tons of relief supplies to the area.

Nov To aid victims of floods in western Panama, USAF helicopters brought in food and relief workers.

1974

Feb U.S. airlifters on rotational duty in Panama airlifted 40,000 pounds of relief supplies to flood victims in Bolivia. Supplies included 8,500 blankets, 10,000 units of penicillin and vitamins, and 10 field kitchens.

May A TAC C–130 located a disabled sloop about 120 miles southwest of Cuba and directed a merchant vessel to render aid.

Jul C–130 airlifters flew disaster relief operations after a massive landslide in Colombia.

Jul A C–5 and C–141 delivered eighty-four tons of supplies, including blankets and cots, to Chile to aid flood victims.

Aug Three MAC C–141s airlifted tents and blankets to Bangladesh to help refugees left homeless by flooding.

Aug Two C–141s delivered thirty-four tons of medical supplies to Burma in the aftermath of severe flooding in that nation.

Sep C–130s flew disaster relief operations after a major hurricane struck Honduras.

Oct In Operation King Grain, USAF airlifters brought in foodstuffs to famine-stricken areas in Chad, Mali, and Mauritania.

Nov USAF airlifters flew flood relief supplies to the Virgin Islands.

Dec U.S. air transports airlifted emergency food supplies to Bangladesh. PACAF aircraft participating in the operation carried over 1,000 tons of supplies during fifty-one missions.

Dec Three C–141s flew ten relief missions to Darwin, Australia, to support relief efforts for the city, which had been devastated by Cyclone Tracy.

1975

Jan At the request of the king of Thailand, U.S. airlifters flew rice and other emergency supplies to northern Thailand. U.S. helicopters distributed these relief supplies to flood-stricken areas.

Feb A C–141 airlifted relief supplies to cyclone-devastated Mauritius in the southwestern Indian Ocean.

May USAF airlifters brought in medical supplies following an outbreak of dengue fever in Guam.

Jul Following flooding in Recife, Brazil, C–130 airlifters carried thirty tons of relief supplies to the region.

Aug After extensive flooding in Romania, USAF C–141s delivered sixty tons of disaster relief supplies to Bucharest.

1976

Feb Following a massive earthquake in Guatemala, USAF aircraft delivered almost 1,000 tons of supplies and emergency support personnel. A TAC mobile fuel unit provided refueling support to rescue helicopters and a SAC U–2 provided reconnaissance to aid in rescue efforts.

Communications equipment rolls off a USAF C–5 Galaxy in Guatemala.

May After a severe earthquake in northeastern Turkey, a C–141 airlifted emergency aid to Aviano, Italy.

May USAF helicopters evacuated 734 Philippine nationals who had been stranded by a major typhoon.

May MAC airlifters flew in relief supplies to residents of Guam following a typhoon.

Jul In support of earthquake relief operations, two C–130s carried twenty tons of supplies from Guam to Indonesia; a C–141 delivered 400 tents.

Oct After an airliner crash that killed 75 and injured more than 100 in Bolivia, a C–141 transported a burn team and medical supplies.

Nov C–141s, C–5s, and C–130s delivered earthquake relief supplies to Turkey following a major quake.

1977

Mar After an earthquake, MAC delivered seven tons of relief supplies to Romania.

Mar Following a collision of two Boeing 747s in the Canary Islands,

MAC aircraft airlifted more than fifty crash victims to medical facilities in the United States.

Apr USAF provided assistance in the Marshall Islands, evacuating personnel after a typhoon struck Eniwetok.

1978

Aug As part of Sudan flood relief, a MAC airlifter delivered twenty-six tons of relief supplies to Khartoum.

Sep A SAC U–2 located a missing fishing boat in the Atlantic.

Sep After Hurricane Greta hit Central America, USAF C–130s airlifted fifty tons of relief cargo to stricken areas in Honduras and Belize.

Oct USAF aircraft rescued twenty-three flood victims in Costa Rica.

Nov Twenty-one C–141s, C–130s, and HH–53s carried the remains of Congressman Leo Ryan, his party, and some 900 followers of the Reverend Jim Jones back to the United States from Jonestown, Guyana.

Nov Five C–141s supported typhoon relief efforts in Sri Lanka.

1979

Mar USAF helicopters, based at Hickam Air Base, Hawaii, rescued nineteen crew members from a sinking Japanese fishing vessel.

Apr After Mount Soufrière volcano erupted on Saint Vincent, Windward Islands, C–130s airlifted thirty tons of relief supplies to aid victims.

Apr Two C–141s airlifted supplies to the Fiji Islands following the ravages of Hurricane Mali.

Apr Osan Air Base helicopters rescued twenty-four persons from a sinking Korean fishing vessel.

Apr A USAF airlifter delivered twenty tons of vegetable seeds to aid starving people in Zaire.

Apr Seven C–141s and one C–130 transported 126 tons of relief supplies to aid earthquake victims in Yugoslavia.

Aug After Hurricane David and Tropical Storm Frederic devastated islands in the Caribbean, USAF airlifters transported more than 2,900 tons of supplies and 1,400 passengers.

Oct The USAF participated in refugee relief operations in Thailand.

Nov Following damage by high waves to the islands of the Majuro Atoll, PACAF aided in relief operations.

Nov After floods, USAF aircraft rescued twenty-seven victims and delivered fresh food and water to Panama.

Dec After an earthquake in Colombia, four USAF C–130s brought in 118 rescue workers and 87 tons of relief equipment.

Dec In response to flooding in Nicaragua, USAF C–130s airlifted at least 117 tons of relief supplies and 247 passengers to stricken areas.

Dec After a flood, a USAF C–130 airlifted fifteen tons of food to Belize.

1980

Jan A C–141 airlifted relief supplies to Mauritius Island in response to the destruction caused by Cyclone Claudette.

Jan USAF airlifters flew typhoon relief supplies to the Marshall Islands.

Jan To assist earthquake victims, C–141s airlifted 700 tents and 1,000 blankets from Italy to the Azores.

Apr The USAF participated in refugee relief operations in Thailand.

Jul An urgent airlift was conducted in Europe for Vice-Consul Richard I. Queen, one of fifty-two Americans held hostage by Iran, released because of illness. A USAF DC–9 flew him from Zurich, Switzerland, to Wiesbaden, West Germany.

Aug After Hurricane Allen, five USAF airlifters brought in sixty-one tons of relief supplies to Haiti and St. Lucia.

Oct After the Coco River flooded, a USAF C–130 brought in forty tons of relief supplies to Nicaragua.

Oct MAC delivered 240 tons of relief supplies after two major earthquakes struck Algeria. Soon afterwards, Algeria moved to act as an intermediary in the Iranian hostage impasse.

Nov Thousands who were rendered homeless by an earthquake in Italy were aided by relief supplies delivered by the USAF. At the request of the Italian government, a SAC U–2 conducted sorties over the Naples area to assess earthquake damage.

Nov USAF aircraft provided relief supplies to the people of Saipan following Typhoon Dinah.

1981

Jan Americans who had been held hostage by Iran were airlifted from Algeria to Germany, and then to the United States.

Feb The USAF provided earthquake relief missions for Greece.

Jul After an earthquake in southern Peru, a USAF C–130 airlifted eight tons of blankets to that nation.

Nov The USAF provided relief supplies for victims of a major earthquake in eastern Turkey.

Dec Six MAC C–141s brought medical supplies from Ramstein Air Base and Italy for earthquake victims in Yemen.

1982

May After a bridge collapsed in Panama, USAF C–130s brought in 381 tons of relief cargo.

Jul A C–130 deployed to Nigeria and set up an airhead to fly daily flights into Chad for famine relief.

Aug USAF airlifters flew refugee relief operations in Lebanon.

Nov After a flood in Tunisia, the USAF brought in relief supplies.

Dec USAF airlifters delivered almost 200 tons of supplies to Yemen for earthquake relief.

1983

Jan When forest fires broke out in Italy, the USAF deployed C–130s equipped for aerial fire-fighting to assist local authorities.

Mar The USAF delivered relief supplies to Fiji islanders recovering from a major cyclone.

Apr After an earthquake, USAF C–130s airlifted thirty-four tons of relief supplies to Colombia.

Apr U.S. nationals who were wounded in an embassy bombing were airlifted from Beirut, Lebanon, to Rhein-Main Air Base near Frankfurt, West Germany.

Jun Two C–130s transported an Army medical relief team from San Antonio, Texas, to El Salvador.

Jul Following a major flood, three USAF C–130s airlifted 170 tons of relief supplies to northwestern Peru.

Jul Two USAF helicopters airlifted ten tons of food and medical supplies to local residents after a flood in Ecuador.

Sep Four C–141s transported eighty-six passengers and thirty-four tons of cargo from Ramstein Air Base to Japan, to assist in the search for the wreckage from Korean Airlines Flight 007. USAF F–15s, KC–135s, E–3As, and RC–135s supported the search operation.

Sep The USAF provided medical supplies to the Truk Islands to combat a cholera outbreak.

Oct Seventy-eight wounded personnel from a Marine barracks bombing in Lebanon were airlifted to medical facilities in the United States and Europe.

Wounded Marines are unloaded at Rhein-Main Air Base following the October 23 bombing of the barracks in Beirut, Lebanon.

Oct MAC flew four C–141 and thirteen C–130 sorties to airlift supplies to Turkey, which had been devastated by an earthquake.

1984

Aug The USAF participated in a typhoon evacuation of Johnston Atoll in the Pacific.

Sep A C–141 delivered three passengers and nine tons of equipment to Kinshasa, Zaire, in support of an AIDS research project.

Sep The USAF provided flood relief to Korea.

Dec Two C–141s flew survivors and bodies of victims from Kuwait after a hijacking attempt.

Dec The USAF provided assistance to refugees in Ethiopia.

1985

Jan When a typhoon left 3,000 homeless, the USAF sent two C–5s and a C–141 to deliver relief supplies to the Fiji Islands.

Jan The USAF again provided assistance to refugees in Ethiopia.

Feb USAF airlifters flew drought relief supplies to Mozambique.

Feb To aid earthquake victims in Argentina, a MAC C–141 brought in 500 tents.

Mar After an earthquake in Chile, a C–5 airlifted sixty tons of plastic tent sheeting to help homeless survivors.

Mar Sudan, Niger, and Mali received famine relief deliveries, which coincided with visits to the region by Vice President George Bush.

Jul A C–141 airlifted thirty-nine male hostages from Syria after a TWA flight was hijacked to Beirut, Lebanon.

Aug A C–5 airlifted three helicopters to Sudan to assist in famine relief operations.

Sep Massive earthquakes wreaked havoc on Mexico City, killing 4,000 people and destroying 2,500 buildings. Airlifters transported 375 tons of cargo to aid rescuers and assist the populace.

Oct The USAF airlifted from Italy to the United States eleven hostages released from the *Achille Lauro* cruise ship.

Oct After mud slides in Puerto Rico, five C–5s, two C–141s, and three C–130s flew in 361 tons of relief supplies and 66 workers.

Nov After a Colombian volcano erupted and unleashed torrents of mud and water, four C–130s delivered fifty tons of supplies and thirty-two tons of fuel for Army helicopters engaged in rescue operations.

Dec The USAF airlifted the dead from an Arrow Air crash in Canada and supported airlift missions.

1986

Feb A C–141 flew Haitian President Jean Claude Duvalier and his family to exile in France.

Feb Helicopters from Clark Air Base extracted Philippines President Ferdinand Marcos and his family from Manila. Marcos was then airlifted to exile in Hawaii aboard a USAF transport aircraft.

Mar The USAF began to deliver $10 million in relief for Afghan refugees in Pakistan, contained in an amendment to the fiscal year 1986 budget.

An Afghan refugee arrives by C–9 in the U.S. for medical treatment.

Apr After a massive meltdown at the Soviet Union's Chernobyl nuclear power plant, MAC aircraft flew eleven air sampling operations.

May Four C–130s airlifted emergency relief supplies and equipment to the typhoon-ravaged Solomon Islands.

Jun After floods, USAF C–130s airlifted twenty-seven tons of relief supplies to Jamaica.

Jul The USAF participated in an airlift of American hostage Rev. Lawrence Jenco from Damascus, Syria, to West Germany, following his release by his captors in Lebanon.

Sep Two C–5s delivered to Manila the largest shipment flown to date under the auspices of the Denton Amendment.

Oct Eighteen MAC airlifters delivered thirty-nine tons of goods, medicine, and other relief supplies to El Salvador after a devastating earthquake.

1987

Feb C–141 aircraft transported more than sixty-six tons of relief supplies to Port Moresby, Papua New Guinea, following Typhoon Uma.

Mar After an earthquake in Ecuador, two USAF C–141s and four C–130s airlifted 107 tons of relief equipment and supplies.

May The USAF airlifted thirty-six dead and wounded from the Arabian Gulf after the attack on the USS *Stark*.

Sep The USAF participated in general relief missions to Chad.

Sep The USAF helped provide general relief to Thailand.

1988

Feb A medical team was transported to Mexico City.

Apr A C–141 airlifted from Bahrain sailors who had been wounded on the *Samuel B. Roberts* when the vessel hit a mine. The transport carried them from the Arabian Gulf to Rhein-Main Air Base, West Germany.

Sep Relief supplies were airlifted to Dhaka, the capital of Bangladesh, after a flood left thirty million people homeless.

Disaster relief supplies are unloaded from a C–5 in Bangladesh.

Sep After a hurricane, the USAF airlifted relief supplies to Jamaica.
Oct USAF airlifters flew hurricane supplies to the Philippines.
Nov The USAF participated in pestilence relief operations in Senegal.
Dec Seven humanitarian aid missions were flown to the USSR to aid survivors of a massive earthquake in Armenia, which left 40,000 dead and 500,000 homeless.

1989

Feb A C–141 airlifted to the United States thirty-seven Soviet Armenian children who had been seriously injured in an earthquake.
Jun A C–141 transported a burn team and supplies to Ufa, Bashkiria, in the USSR to treat one hundred burned children.

Medical equipment and supplies for the burn team are unloaded at Ufa.

Aug USAF airlifters deployed search and rescue helicopters to locate Congressman Mickey Leland's aircraft, which had disappeared in Ethiopia. Congressman Leland and fifteen other passengers were killed in this crash and USAF airlifters returned their bodies to the United States.
Sep The USAF participated in a medical airlift to Liberia.
Sep Fifty-one C–5s, fifty-three C–141s, twenty-three C–130s, and one KC–10 transported 1,365 passengers and 3,938 tons of humanitarian cargo to Puerto Rico, St. Thomas, and St. Croix in the wake of Hurricane Hugo.
Oct A C–5 delivered large quantities of excess Department of Defense property to Sierra Leone, Liberia, Niger, Chad, and Cameroon in a humanitarian special assignment airlift mission, Africa-2.

1990

Feb After a cyclone struck Western Samoa and rendered 12,000-15,000 people homeless, a C–5 transported disaster relief supplies and personnel to the stricken area. A C–130 aided in search and rescue operations.

Apr A MAC C–141 transported Robert Polhill, a freed American hostage who had been held in Lebanon, from Damascus, Syria, to Rhein-Main Air Base, West Germany. He was then flown by helicopter to the U.S. military hospital at Wiesbaden.

Freed hostage Robert Polhill walks off a C–141 at Rhein-Main Air Base.

Jun A MAC rescue team operating from a C–141 dropped a canister containing medical supplies to an American citizen stricken with asthma aboard a private sailing vessel between Peru and Hawaii. The ailing man's wife retrieved the parcel, dropped within ten feet of the vessel's bow, and successfully administered the medication.

Jul After a major earthquake devastated the northern Philippines, PACAF deployed construction personnel, opened hospitals, and supplied other humanitarian aid.

Sep When heavy rains flooded South Korea, the 38th Air Rescue Squadron saved twenty-four people from flood waters.

Dec The 38th Air Rescue Squadron rescued twenty-two crew members of a Panamanian vessel that ran aground off Korea.

1991

Mar A C–5 delivered sixty-five tons of medical equipment to Romania. In addition to excess Department of Defense property, the flight carried cargo privately collected by Project Handclasp. Additional humanitarian flights followed.

Apr Following a cholera epidemic in Peru, MAC C–5 missions brought in 200 tons of medical supplies.

Apr In the wake of the Gulf War, Iraqi dictator Saddam Hussein's elite Republican Guards put down a rebellion by the Kurdish people in the northern part of the country. In April 1991 the Air Force began Operation Provide Comfort, which brought relief supplies to the Kurds.

One of thousands of Kurdish refugees at the Isikveren camp.

May MAC established a strategic airlift to Bangladesh to deliver 738 passengers and 832 tons of food to alleviate suffering caused by Cyclone Marion. Additionally, an intratheater airlift delivered food from depots established in-country.

May TAC deployed forces as well as Harvest Eagle and Harvest Bare equipment to Guantanamo (GTMO, pronounced "Gitmo") Bay Naval Station, Cuba, in support of Operation GTMO, providing humanitarian relief to Haitian migrants.

May A C–5 delivered twenty-five tons of medical supplies to Quito, Ecuador.

Jun In the largest airlift evacuation since the war in Southeast Asia, MAC transport and civil aircraft moved 52,018 PACAF personnel and their dependents from Clark Air Base and Subic Bay Naval Station in the Philippines to the United States following the volcanic eruption of Mount Pinatubo.

Jun A MAC C–141 delivered medical supplies in what was the first flight of an American military aircraft into Mongolia.

Jul MAC transport aircraft delivered food and relief supplies to aid miners as well as some of Mother Teresa's relief organizations in Tiranë, Albania.

Jul In response to drought and the consequences of civil war, MAC airlifted seventy tons of cargo to N'Djamena, Chad.

Aug MAC C–141s began transporting hostages released in Damascus, Syria, from captivity in Lebanon.

Aug Following flooding, a MAC C–5 delivered blankets and medical supplies to Shanghai for distribution in central and eastern China.

Oct A MAC C–5 delivered relief supplies following flooding in Mongolia.

Oct Two MAC C–5s delivered donated medical supplies as well as excess Defense Department blankets and equipment to Kiev, Ukraine.

Nov The devastation caused by three typhoons beginning in November led to the delivery of relief supplies by MAC and PACAF aircraft to Guam and the Marshalls.

Nov MAC aircraft joined Alaska Air National Guard and Canadian Forces aircraft to rescue fourteen survivors of a crash of a Canadian C–130 near the North Pole.

Dec Two MAC C–5s made the first direct airlift of food aid to the Soviet Union.

1992

Feb MAC and USAFE began delivering food and medical supplies to the Commonwealth of Independent States, the former Soviet Union, in Operation Provide Hope. The Air Force designated a follow-on operation "Provide Hope II."

Mar Within forty-eight hours of a devastating earthquake in Turkey, MAC C–130s began delivering food, water, and clothing. Heavy equipment to aid in rescue work was also brought in later.

Apr Following extensive fires in oil fields in Uzbekistan, MAC C–141s delivered specialized fire-fighting equipment from the United States.

Jul Operation Provide Promise, a series of relief flights into Sarajevo, began on July 3, 1992, and became the longest sustained humanitarian airlift in history. By May 1995 U.S. aircraft had delivered more than 55,953 metric tons of food, medicine, and supplies. They also had dropped more than 18,002 metric tons of relief into areas of Bosnia-Herzegovina that United Nations convoys could not reach by land.

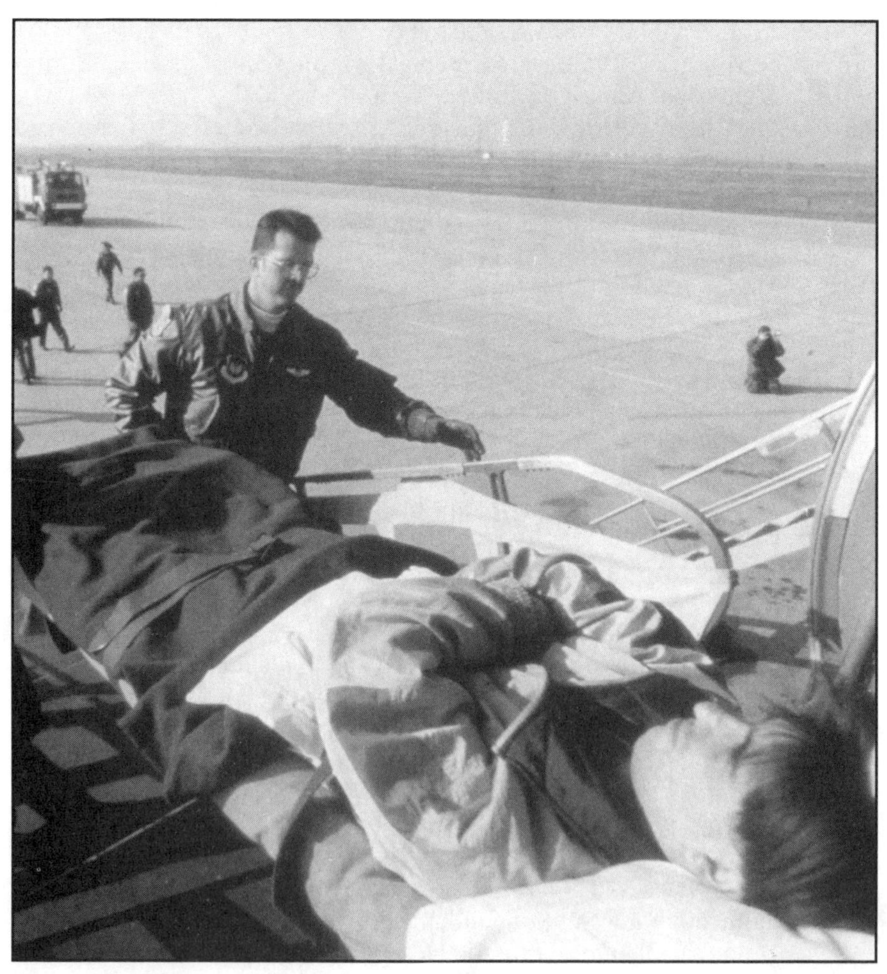

A casualty of the conflict in Bosnia is airlifted to the U.S. for treatment.

Croatian corn seeds were airdropped over Bosnia during Provide Promise.

Aug AMC aircraft began flying Operation Provide Relief missions to Somalia and Kenya to aid Somalis threatened by starvation due to anarchy in their country and a prolonged drought.

Aug After devastation brought by Typhoon Omar, AMC and PACAF relief missions brought cargo and people to Guam to aid the island's recovery.

Sep An AMC C–141 airlifted seventy children who suffered from the effects of the Chernobyl nuclear accident of 1986, transporting them from Minsk, Belarus, to Belgium for medical treatment.

Nov AMC C–5 and C–141 missions delivered 236 metric tons of flour at the urgent request of the Armenian government to alleviate a severe bread shortage.

Dec In Operation Restore Hope, AMC and ACC airlifters delivered food, medicine, logistical support, and other cargo to Somalia, while AMC tankers built an "airbridge" over the Atlantic to keep supplies flowing. These activities supported American ground forces who were rescuing starving Somalis from a country which had fallen into anarchy.

Part of the daily audience watching U.S. Marines at work in Somalia.

1994

May Following an outbreak of massacres in Rwanda, AMC mounted Operation Support Hope, which flew 1,220 airlift sorties and delivered 15 tons of humanitarian aid to this country. More than 400,000 refugees fled to neighboring nations, and civilian and military aircraft also made relief flights to Burundi, Uganda, Tanzania, and Zaire.

Notes

1. Mauer Mauer, *Aviation in the U.S. Army, 1919-1939* (Washington, D.C., 1987), 143, 144.
2. George N. Dubina and Margaret M. Dixon, *Air University History Chronology, 1910-1957* (Maxwell Air Force Base, Ala., 1964), 90-94; Office of Information, Headquarters Air University, *Fifty Years of Airlift History at Maxwell AFB, 1910-1960* (Maxwell Air Force Base, Ala., 1960); Jerome A. Ennels, "Maxwell Flood Relief, 1929," *Air Power History*, Spring 1989, 30-35.
3. *Air Force Times*, Dec. 1, 1965, 9; *Air Corps Newsletter*, Jan. 25, 1932, 9; Ernest LaRue Jones Papers, Air Force Historical Research Agency (hereafter AFHRA).
4. Mauer Mauer, *Air Force Combat Units of World War II* (Washington, D.C., 1983), 38.
5. Mauer Mauer, *Combat Squadrons of the Air Force, World War II* (Washington, D.C., 1969), 106, 188, 192, 320.
6. History of the I Bomber Command, vol. 2; History of the 2d Bombardment Wing, supporting document, both AFHRA.
7. Clive Ponting, *Armageddon* (New York and London, 1995), 355.
8. Ibid.; 2d Air Division lineage and honors history, attachment 2, AFHRA.
9. Ponting, *Armageddon*, 355; Col. Harold F. Nufer, draft article, "Operation Chowhound: A Precedent for Post-World War II Humanitarian Airlift," AFHRA.
10. Walter LaFeber, *America, Russia, and the Cold War 1945-1990* (New York, 1991), 54-57, 58-63. On the reorganization of the Department of Defense and on the emergence of the Air Force as a separate service, see Steven L. Rearden, *History of the Office of the Secretary of Defense: The Formative Years 1947-1950* (Washington, D.C., 1984), and Herman S. Wolk, *Planning and Organizing the Postwar Air Force 1943-1947* (Washington, D.C., 1984).
11. LaFeber, *America, Russia, and the Cold War*, 77; History of the First Airlift Task Force, Nov. 1948, Dec. 1948, and Sept. 1949, and History of the Combined Airlift Task Force, Jan.-Aug. 1949, both AFHRA; Lucius D. Clay, *Decision in Germany* (New York, 1950), 367, 381-83, 390; Roger D. Launius, "The Berlin Airlift: Constructive Air Power," *Air Power History*, Spring 1989, 9-22.
12. LaFeber, *America, Russia, and the Cold War*, 84.
13. There are many useful books on the Korean War, including the U.S. Army and Marine Corps official histories; Clay Blair, *The Forgotten War: America in Korea 1950-1953* (New York and Toronto, 1987); and John Toland, *In Mortal Combat: Korea, 1950-1953* (New York, 1991). For an exhaustive treatment of USAF operations, see Robert F. Futrell, *The United States Air Force in Korea, 1950-1953* (Washington, D.C., 1983).
14. History of the Pacific Division, Military Air Transport Service, Jan.-June 1953, History of the 315th Air Division, Jan.-June 1953, History of the Military Air Transport Service, July-Dec. 1953, all AFHRA; A. G. Thompson, *The Greatest Airlift: The Story of Combat Cargo* (Tokyo, 1954), 455-64.
15. History of the Military Air Transport Service, July-Dec. 1952, AFHRA; "Airlift for Allah," *Time*, Sept. 8, 1952, 32.
16. Thompson, *The Greatest Airlift,* 314-22; History of the 483rd Troop Carrier Wing, Jan.-June 1953, AFHRA.
17. History of the Atlantic Division, Air Transportation Command, 1949, and History of the Continental Air Command, Dec. 1, 1948-Dec. 31, 1949, both AFHRA; "Davis-Monthan C–47 Drops Hay at Cowboy's Direction," *Air Force Times*, Feb. 12, 1949, 12; "Homecoming Beacon at Ely Helps Haylift Pilots," *Air Force Times*, Feb. 26, 1949, 1, 20.

18. History of the 315th Air Division, July-Dec. 1954, AFHRA; "C–124s Deliver Medical Supplies to East Pakistan," *Air Force Times*, Aug. 21, 1954, 27.

19. History of the Military Air Transport Service, July-Dec. 1954, AFHRA; "MATS Winds Up Airlift of 506 French Wounded," *Air Force Times*, Aug. 7, 1954, 32.

20. History of the 315th Air Division, Jan.-June 1955, AFHRA.

21. LaFeber, *America, Russia, and the Cold War*, 185-89; History of the 322d Air Division, July-Dec. 1956 and Jan.-June 1957, and attached Mar. 1957 *Fleetliner* magazine, 3, 9, all AFHRA; "Food, Supplies Rushed to Aid Hungarians," *Air Force Times*, Nov. 10, 1956, 10.

22. History of the 322d Air Division, July-Dec. 1956, and traffic division appendix; History of the 60th Troop Carrier Wing, July-Dec. 1956; History of the 317th Troop Carrier Wing, July-Dec. 1956; History of the 465th Troop Carrier Wing, July-Dec. 1956, all AFHRA.

23. History of the Military Air Transport Service, Jan.-June 1957, AFHRA; Milton Krims, "Operation Safe Haven—Air Bridge to Freedom," *Air Force Magazine*, June 1957, 68, 71-72, 75-76, 80, 83-84, 87.

24. *Department of State Bulletin*, June 13, 1960, 966-67; "Chile: The 10,000-Mile Disaster," *Newsweek*, May 30, 1960, 56; "The Earth Shook, Seas Heaved, Winds Blew," *Newsweek*, June 6, 1960, 68-69; "Chile: The Deadly Earth," *Time*, June 6, 1960, 32.

25. History of the Caribbean Air Command, Jan.-June 1960, and Caribbean Command After Action Report, Chilean Disaster Relief Operation, May-July 1960, both AFHRA; Stanley Ulanoff, *MATS: The Story of the Military Air Transport Service* (New York, 1964), 115; Dick Burkard, *Military Airlift Command Historical Handbook, 1941-1984* (Scott Air Force Base, Ill., 1984), 5.

26. History of the United States Air Forces in Europe, July-Dec. 1960, and History of the Western Transport Air Force, July-Dec. 1960, both AFHRA.

27. History of the Western Air Transport Air Force, July-Dec. 1961, and History of the 315th Air Division, July-Dec. 1961, both AFHRA.

28. History of the United States Air Forces in Europe, July-Dec. 1962 and Jan.-June 1963; History of the Military Air Transport Service, July 1962-June 1963; History of the 322d Air Division, July-Dec. 1962, all AFHRA.

29. History of the Eastern Transport Air Force, July-Dec. 1962, and History of the Western Transport Air Force, July-Dec. 1962, both AFHRA.

30. History of the Eastern Transport Air Force, Jan.-June 1964 and July-Dec. 1964; Chronology of the 322d Air Division, Apr. 1964-Dec. 1966; and History of the 322d Air Division, July-Dec. 1964, all AFHRA; Timothy A. Fuhrman, "Pakistan Airlift 64," *Airlift Operations Review*, Jan. 1982, 25-27.

31. History of the Thirteenth Air Force, Jan.-Dec. 1964, AFHRA; "Military Choppers Assist Vietnamese Flood Victims," *Air Force Times*, Dec. 30, 1964, 16.

32. History of the Military Air Transport Service, Jan.-June 1964, and History of the Tactical Air Command, Jan.-June 1964, both AFHRA; "Military Helps Alaska Recover from Quake," *Air Force Times*, Apr. 15, 1964, 2.

33. Sixth Air Force Reserve Region Final Report, Domestic Emergency, Northern California/Oregon Flood, Air Force Reserve History Office files, Robins Air Force Base, Ga.; History of the Sixth Air Force Reserve Region, Jan.-June 1965, AFHRA; "Reservists (Again) Aid Disaster Victims," *Air Reservist*, Feb. 1965, 6-7.

34. There are many survey histories of the Vietnam War, including George C. Herring, *America's Longest War: The United States and Vietnam, 1950-1975* (Philadelphia, 1986); Dave Richard Palmer, *Summons of the Trumpet: A History of the Vietnam War From a*

Military Man's Viewpoint (New York, 1984); and Ray Bonds, ed. *The Vietnam War: The Illustrated History of the Conflict in Southeast Asia* (New York, 1979).

35. History of the Eastern Transport Air Force, Jan.-Dec. 1965, AFHRA.

36. History of the Twenty-First Air Force, Fiscal Year 1971, AFHRA; "U.S. Choppers Aid Pakistan," *Air Force Times*, Dec. 30, 1964, 16. Earlier the same year more than twenty-five Air Force planes brought mobile hospitals, medical personnel, and supplies to Jordan after civil strife had erupted in that country. History of the United States Air Forces in Europe, Fiscal Year 1971, AFHRA; "TAC C–130s Log Far-Flung Relief," *Air Force Times*, Mar. 10, 1971, 26.

37. History of the Tactical Air Command, Fiscal Year 1972, and Military Airlift Command News Release No. 6-28-71-244, both AFHRA; "Mission of Mercy Airlifts Thousands," *Air Force Times*, Aug. 18, 1971, 32.

38. History of Headquarters USAF Directorate of Operations, July-Dec. 1973; History of the Military Airlift Command, July 1973-June 1974; History of Tactical Air Command, July 1973-June 1974, all AFHRA; "Pakistan Flood," *Air Reservist*, Oct. 1973, 2; "Pakistan," *Facts on File*, 1973, 753, C-1.

39. History of the Military Airlift Command, July 1974-Dec. 1975, AFHRA; Maj. George J. Klazynski, "The Airlift Role in Operations Babylift and New Life," Air University Library Manuscript, M-43122-U K 632a; "Project New Life," *Air Reservist*, July 1975, 7.

40. History of the Air Force Reserve, Jan.-Dec. 1977, AFHRA; "California Fires," *Air Reservist*, Oct. 1977, 11; History of the Fourth Air Force, Jan.-Dec. 1979, AFHRA; Lt. Kathleen Berg, "Summer Scrapbook '79," *Air Reservist*, Oct. 1979, 19; Sgt. Pat Vick, "Forest Firefighters," *Air Reservists*, Nov. 1979, 16; History of the Air Force Reserve, Oct. 1986-Sept. 1987, Air Force Reserve History Office files, Robins Air Force Base, Ga.

41. History of the Military Airlift Command, July 1974-Dec. 1975; and History of the Western Air Force Reserve Region, July-Dec. 1975, both AFHRA; Lt. Col. Bob Zehring and A1C Allen D. Childers, "The Fire Fighters," *Air Reservist*, Oct. 1975, 4-5; "ANG C–130s Fight Forest Fire," *Air Force Times*, June 30, 1986, 40; "The Air National Guard by Major Command Assignment," *Air Force Magazine*, May 1988, 169.

42. History of the Tactical Air Command, Fiscal Year 1973, July 1973-June 1974 and July 1974-June 1975; History of HQ USAF Directorate of Operations, July-Dec. 1973 and July-Dec. 1974, all AFHRA.

43. Air Force White Paper, "45 Years of Global Reach and Global Power: The United States Air Force and National Security, 1947-1992, A Historical Perspective" (Washington, D.C., 1992), 49.

44. History of the Military Airlift Command, 1976 and 1977; History of the United States Air Forces in Europe, 1976, all AFHRA.

45. History of the Military Airlift Command, 1978 and 1979; History of the 322d Airlift Division, 23 Jan. 1978-31 Dec. 1979, all AFHRA; Bonner Day, "Exodus from Iran," *Air Force Magazine*, June 1979, 72-74.

46. History of the Military Airlift Command, 1986-1987, AFHRA; TSgt. David Masko, "Humanitarian Airlift," *Airman*, Feb. 1992, 16-19.

47. John W. Leland, "Humanitarian Airlift to Soviet Armenia" (Scott Air Force Base, Ill., 1990).

48. "45 Years of Global Reach and Global Power," 49; Robert Van Elsberg, "In the Eye of the Storm," *Citizen Airman*, Jan. 1990, 26-29; "Department of the Air Force Presentation to the Committee on Appropriations, Subcommittee on Defense, U.S. House of Representatives," Apr. 1990, 12; Julia Malone, "Bush Orders Troops to St. Croix," *Atlanta Journal and Constitution*, Sept. 21, 1989, A1, A6; "AF Crews React to Help Hurricane

Victims," *Maxwell-Gunter Dispatch*, Sept. 29, 1989, 6; "Southern Bases Suffer Through Hugo," *Maxwell-Gunter Dispatch*, Oct. 6, 1989, 6; "Air Force Suffers From, Responds to Hugo," *Maxwell-Gunter Dispatch*, Oct. 20, 1989, 6.

49. The literature on the Gulf War includes Lawrence Freedman and Efraim Karsh, *The Gulf Conflict, 1990-1991: Diplomacy and War in the New World Order* (Princeton, N.J., 1993), a scholarly work which focuses on diplomatic issues, and Rick Atkinson, *Crusade: The Untold Story of the Gulf War* (Boston, 1993), a journalistic effort which emphasizes the military conduct of the war. On the air campaign, see Richard P. Hallion, *Storm Over Iraq: Air Power and the Gulf War* (Washington, D.C., and London, 1992), and Thomas A. Keaney and Eliot A. Cohen, *Gulf War Air Power Survey Summary Report* (Washington, D.C., 1993).

50. Mary Beth Sheridan, "U.S. Military Sending Massive Aid to Kurds," *Montgomery Advertiser*, Apr. 13, 1991, 1A, 12A; Donald B. Rice, "Reshaping for the Future," Air Force White Paper (Washington, D.C., 1991), 25; SSgt. David P. Masko, "U.S. Allies Continue Kurdish Aid," *Maxwell-Gunter Dispatch*, May 17, 1991, 6; "Kurd Relief Effort Ended Monday," *Maxwell-Gunter Dispatch*, July 19, 1991; *Air Force Message*, Sept. 9, 1992, 7.

51. On the end of the Cold War, see Louis J. Halle, *The Cold War as History* (New York, 1991), and LeFeber, *America, Russia, and the Cold War,* 316-35.

52. John W. Leland, "Operation Provide Hope, Feb. 1992-Apr. 1993" (Scott Air Force Base, Ill., 1993).

53. "Provide Promise Milestone," *Air Force Magazine*, Dec. 1993, 15.

54. Messages from Air Force News Service, Kelly Air Force Base, Tex., Feb. 17, 1993, 5-8, and Mar. 12, 1993, 4-8; TSgt. David P. Masko, "Relief Mission Continues," *Maxwell-Gunter Dispatch,* Mar. 12, 1993, 6; "Community Honors 908th for Humanitarian Efforts," *Maxwell-Gunter Dispatch,* Oct. 8, 1993, 6; "U.S. Fortifies Bosnia Support," *Air Force Magazine*, Oct. 1993, 16.

55. "45 Years of Global Reach and Global Power," 51; Julie Bird, "Airlift Gives Somalians a Taste of Hope," *Air Force Times*, Sept. 14, 1992, 16, 18.

56. "45 Years of Global Reach and Global Power," 50; Rice, "Reshaping for the Future," 25; "MAC Speeds Aid to Bangladesh," *Airman*, June 1991, 10; Edith Lederer, "U.S. Relief Effort Just Beginning," *Montgomery Advertiser*, May 18, 1991; "U.S. Delivers 265 Tons of Supplies to Bangladesh," *Montgomery Advertiser*, May 19, 1991; "Storm Toll at 100,000, Still Rising," *Alabama Journal*, May 3, 1991; "U.S. Begins Bangladesh Relief Effort," *Alabama Journal*, May 15, 1991.

57. "45 Years of Global Reach and Global Power," 50; Rice, "Reshaping for the Future," 25.

58. Messages from Air Force News, Kelly Air Force Base, Tex., Sept. 2, 1992, 4-7, and Sept. 9, 1992, 5; Marcia Dunn, "Federal Troops Bring Supplies to Weary Hurricane Victims," *Montgomery Advertiser*, Aug. 29, 1992, 1A, 6A; SSgt. Gary Quesenberry, "Local Reserve Squadron Spearheads Homestead Humane Relief Effort," *Maxwell-Gunter Dispatch*, Sept. 11, 1992, 1, 12-13.

59. "AMC Helps Flooded Areas," *Air Force Magazine*, Oct. 1993, 17; "Midwest Flood '93," *Airman*, Oct. 1993, 17.